MW01486824

SUPERSTARS
OF THE
SEATTLE
SEAHAWKS

by Allan Morey

AMICUS | AMICUS INK

Amicus High Interest and Amicus Ink are imprints of Amicus
P.O. Box 1329, Mankato, MN 56002
www.amicuspublishing.us

Library of Congress Cataloging-in-Publication Data
Names: Morey, Allan, author.
Title: Superstars of the Seattle Seahawks / by Allan Morey.
Description: Mankato, MN : Amicus, 2019. | Series: Pro sports superstars NFL |
Includes index. | Audience: K to grade 3.
Identifiers: LCCN 2017057758 (print) | LCCN 2017059317 (ebook) | ISBN 9781681514932
(pdf) | ISBN 9781681514116 (library binding) | ISBN 9781681523316 (pbk.)
Subjects: LCSH: Seattle Seahawks (Football team)--Biography--Juvenile literature. |
Seattle Seahawks (Football team)--History--Juvenile literature. | Football players--
United States--Biography--Juvenile literature.
Classification: LCC GV956.S4 (ebook) | LCC GV956.S4 M665 2019 (print) | DDC
796.332/6409797772--dc23 LC record available at https://lccn.loc.gov/2017057758

Photo Credits: All photos from Associated Press except AP/Greg Trott cover, Allen Kee
12–13; Getty Images/Jonathan Ferrey 4–5, Mike Powell 10–11, Otto Greule Jr 14–15

Series Designer: Veronica Scott
Book Designer: Peggie Carley
Photo Researcher: Holly Young

Printed in China
HC 10 9 8 7 6 5 4 3 2 1
PB 10 9 8 7 6 5 4 3 2 1

TABLE OF CONTENTS

GET TO KNOW THE SEAHAWKS

The Seahawks joined the **NFL** in 1976. They are from Seattle, Washington. In 2014, they won their first Super Bowl.

Here are some of the team's star players.

The Seahawks' Ring of Honor includes successful players who hold amazing records.

JIM ZORN

Jim Zorn was the Seahawks' first **quarterback.** He led them from 1976 to 1984.

Zorn is in the Seahawks' **Ring of Honor.** He is one of the team's greatest players.

STEVE LARGENT

Steve Largent played from
1976 to 1989. He is a Seahawks
legend. He caught more passes
than any other Seahawks
player. He holds the team
record for receiving yards.

KENNY EASLEY

Kenny Easley was great at defending passes. In 1984, he made 10 **interceptions**. He was also the Defensive Player of the Year. Easley joined the Pro Football Hall of Fame in 2017.

CORTEZ KENNEDY

Cortez Kennedy was a tough tackler. In 1992, he had 14 **sacks**. He earned Defensive Player of the Year honors. Kennedy played in eight **Pro Bowls**.

Walter Jones's jersey number (71) was retired in 2010. No other Seahawk can wear that number.

WALTER JONES

Walter Jones played from 1997 to 2008. He was one of the best blockers in the NFL. Jones played in nine Pro Bowls. He is in the Pro Football Hall of Fame.

RUSSELL WILSON

Russell Wilson plays quarterback. He passes the ball. But he is also a speedy rusher. In 2014, he ran for 849 yards. He scored six rushing touchdowns. Wilson helped the Seahawks win the Super Bowl in 2014.

EARL THOMAS

Earl Thomas joined the Seahawks in 2010. He is a team leader on **defense**. He tackles. He knocks down passes. Thomas helped lead the team to its first Super Bowl win.

Thomas is part of the Seahawks' Legion of Boom. This group of defenders is one of the best in the NFL.

YOUNG STAR

Shaquill Griffin was a **rookie** in 2017. He is already showing great defensive skills.

The Seahawks have had many great players. Who will be their next star?

TEAM FAST FACTS

Founded: 1976

Home Stadium: CenturyLink Field (Seattle, Washington)

Super Bowl Titles: 1 (2014)

Nicknames: Hawks, Legion of Boom (for the defensive backs)

Hall of Fame Players: 9 including Kenny Easley, Walter Jones, Cortez Kennedy, and Steve Largent

WORDS TO KNOW

defense – a group of players who try to stop the other team from scoring

interception – when the opponent catches a pass

NFL – National Football League; the league pro football players play in

Pro Bowl – the NFL's all-star game

quarterback – a player whose main jobs are to lead the offense and throw passes

Ring of Honor – a group of people important to the Seahawks' history

rookie – a first year player

sack – a play during which the quarterback is tackled for a loss of yards

LEARN MORE

Books

Bodden. Valerie. *Football*. Mankato, Minn: Creative Education, 2016.

Burgess, Zack. *Meet the Seattle Seahawks*. Chicago: Norwood House Press, 2017.

Schuh, Mari. *Russell Wilson*. North Mankato, Minn: Capstone Press, 2016.

Websites

Seattle Seahawks—Official Site
http://www.seahawks.com
Watch video clips and view photos of the Seattle Seahawks.

NFL.com
http://nfl.com
Check out pictures and your favorite football players' stats.

NFL Rush
http://www.nflrush.com
Play games and learn how to be a part of NFL PLAY 60.

Every effort has been made to ensure that these websites are appropriate for children. However, because of the nature of the Internet, it is impossible to guarantee that these sites will remain active indefinitely or that their contents will not be altered.

INDEX